BOLD KIDS

CHILDREN'S AMERICAN LOCAL HISTORY BOOK

No part of this book may be reproduced or used in any way or form or by any means whether electronic or mechanical, this means that you cannot record or photocopy any material ideas or tips that are provided in this book.
Copyright 2022

All images in this book have been reproduced with the knowledge and prior consent of the artists concerned, and no responsibility is accepted by producer, publisher, or printer for any infringement of copyright or otherwise, arising from the contents of this publication.

Minnesota

There are a lot of interesting facts about Minnesota for kids that can spark your imagination and inspire your road trip. This book will give you some of the most fascinating facts about the state of Minnesota.

Minnesota

It will also help you learn more about the history, culture, and traditions of this great American state. Here are some of the top Minnesota facts for kids to know. It's also a great place to visit and learn about its many attractions.

minnesota

The state was first settled by Native Americans, but it was only in 1858 that the state became the 32nd state. It is the only Midwestern territory to be a Union state, and was the first to volunteer soldiers in the Civil War.

Minnesota

There are several fun facts about Minnesota for kids to learn about. These facts can be fun and educational for kids. You can include them in your road trip itinerary. The facts below will help you learn more about Minnesota and make your trip even more enjoyable.

Minnesota

In addition to being the state capital, Minnesota is home to many famous people. Prince and Bob Dylan were born in the state, as was Paul Bunyan and Babe the blue ox. In addition, Minnesota has a rich history of music.

Minnesota

In fact, it was the first state to recognize a major pop star. You can also learn about the state's flowers and trees. There are many places to see in Minnesota.

Minnesota

If you're traveling with kids, you can also teach them about the state's history. The University of Minnesota was the first to perform an open heart surgery, as well as the first bone marrow transplant in the United States.

Minnesota

In addition to famous people, Minnesota is also home to the Mayo Clinic, an institute of high learning and discovery. The Minnesota River is named after the river that flows through the state, the Minnesota. It has more lakes than the combined states of California, Florida, and Hawaii.

Minnesota

If you want to learn more about the state of Minnesota, you can take a look at the country's famous people. It was home to many artists, including Bob Dylan, and the legendary singer Prince. The Twin Cities are also home to a lot of Fortune 500 companies.

Minnesota

The mall in Bloomington is the largest mall in the U.S. and is the size of 78 football fields. The state's Metrodome is the only stadium to host both the World Series and the NCAA Final Four Basketball Championship.

Minnesota

It's a good idea to educate yourself and your children about the history of Minnesota. The best way to do this is to visit the state's attractions and museums. These will make your children more interested in the state.

Minnesota

You can also learn about the famous inventions of Minnesotans. Some of these include the famous roller skates and Scotch tape. If you're traveling with kids, they'll find out the state's flag, flower, and tree.

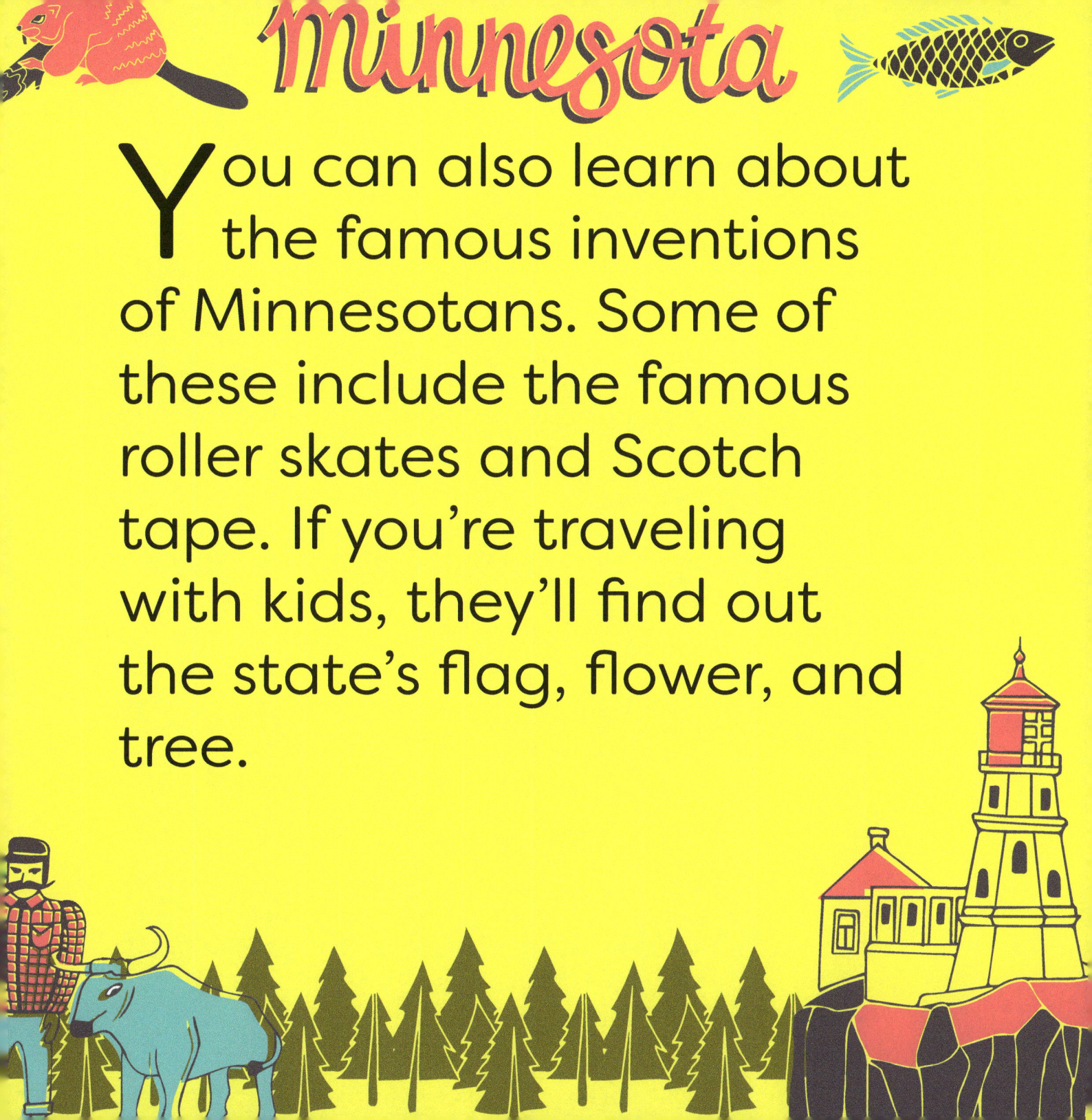

Minnesota

Besides being home to the state's famous people, Minnesota is also home to some amazing inventions. You might be surprised to learn that the world's largest manufacturing plant is in the state of Minnesota.

Minnesota

The company also invented the first ice hockey boot and three inline wheels. The technology has helped the world become a much better place. Other fascinating Minnesota facts for kids include the state's famous rivers, lakes, and forests.

Minnesota

The state of Minnesota is located in the Midwestern United States and borders Canada. The state is a neighbor to Lake Superior and Canada and has many natural and cultural attractions.

Minnesota

The name of the state comes from the Dakota language and means "sky-tinted water." Eagle Mountain is the highest point in Minnesota. The Common Loon is the state bird. Its motto is "Star of the North".

Minnesota

Among other things, Minnesota is home to some of the most interesting laws.

Minnesota

Its skunk law prohibits teasing skunks. Its population has one recreational boat per six residents. Lastly, Minnesota is home to the first public library in the country to create a special section for children.

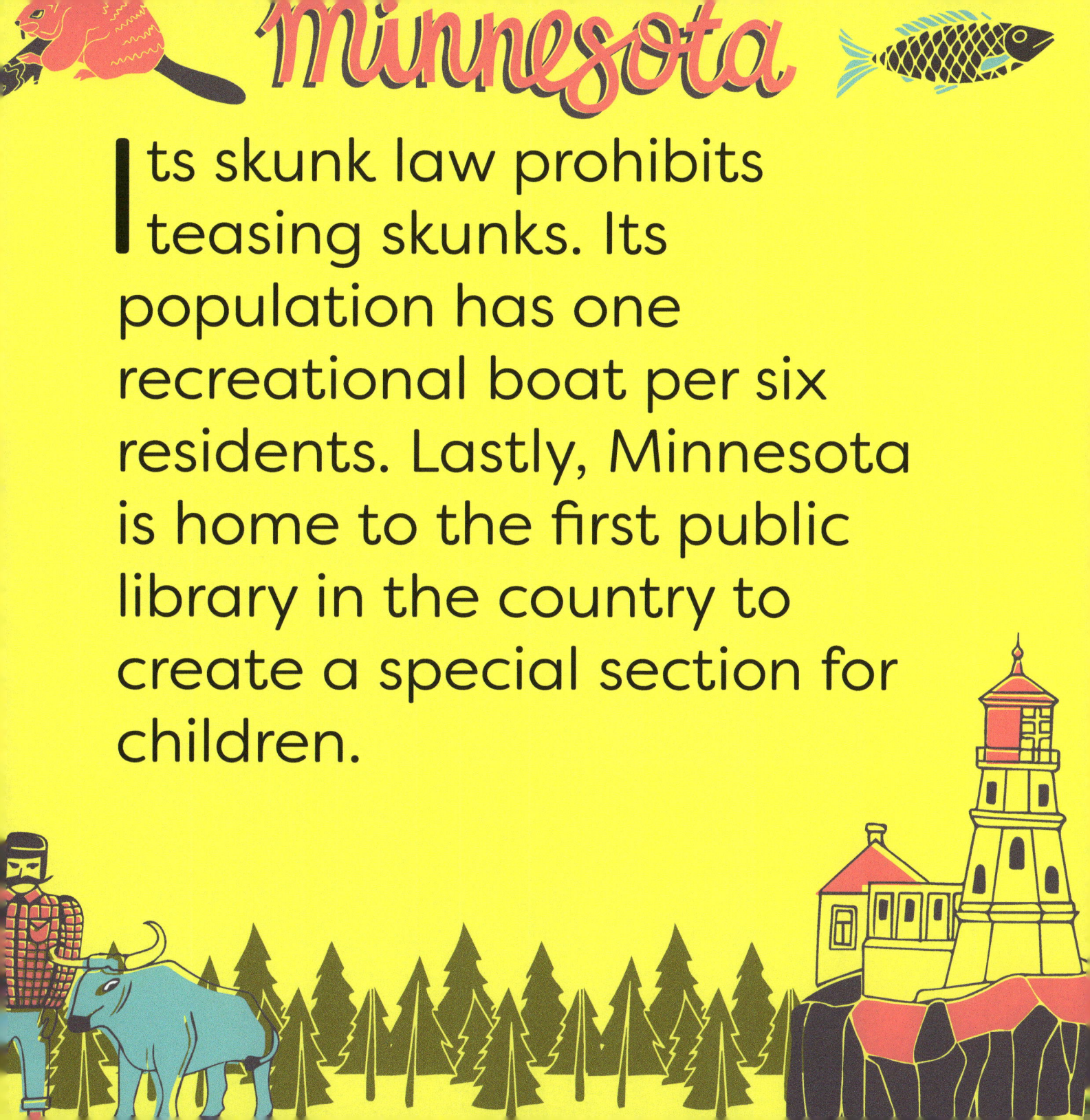

Milton Keynes UK
Ingram Content Group UK Ltd.
UKHW050347170823
426995UK00007B/33